Imagery Training
a guide for sports coaches and performers

Preface

Many factors contribute to sports performance. In addition to the physical, technical and strategic demands of sport, performers must be able to remain focused, maintain emotional control, sustain self-confidence, and constantly apply themselves in both training and competition. In your own sport, you will undoubtedly be able to recognise the mental demands placed on performers. Meeting these demands may be relatively easy when things are going well but less so during times of difficulty (eg poor form, distractions, injury). Coaches typically identify a range of mental qualities that seem to underpin successful sports performance – qualities encompassed in the 4Cs: commitment, confidence, concentration and control.

These qualities can be nurtured and strengthened through mental skills training techniques and strategies such as relaxation, the development of routines, positive self-talk and imagery. Successful performers have been shown to possess and frequently use effective imagery skills – for example, to build self-confidence, focus concentration and regain emotional control. This booklet, *Imagery Training: a guide for sports coaches and performers*, will help coaches and performers develop and use imagery, both in training and competition.

It includes 18 exercises to help you develop the technique and use it effectively in a variety of settings. This booklet will help you to be able to:

- explain what imagery is, why and how it works
- develop your own imagery skills by following a series of exercises to improve clarity and control
- determine when and how to use it in training and competition.

Ideally it should be used in conjunction with the scUK Develop your Coaching workshop, *Imagery Training*[1].

1   For details of all **sports coach UK** workshops running in your area, visit www.sportscoachuk.org/improve/workshop/index.htm or contact the **scUK** Business Support Centre on 01509-226130.

1095084

£24:71

Key to symbols used in the text:

 Exercise to do at home

  Exercise to do in training

 Video camera

 Video playback

 Helper

Stopwatch

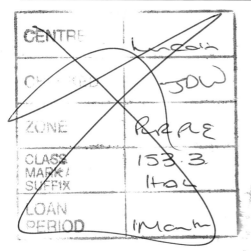
Throughout this pack, the pronouns he, she, him, her and so on are interchangeable and intended to be inclusive of both men and women. It is important in sport, as elsewhere, that men and women have equal status and opportunities.

Contents

SECTION ONE
Imagery: What It Is, Why It Works and How to Use It

Introduction

The field of mental skills training is still relatively new to many coaches and performers, although the importance of the mind in sport has been recognised for many years. Sport involves a mind game as well as a physical performance and peak performance will remain an unobtainable dream for most performers, without developing qualities such as the 4Cs:

- Commitment (ie will to win, toughness)
- Control of emotions (eg of anxiety, anger, frustration)
- Concentration (ie focus)
- Confidence (ie positive attitude, self-belief).

You are probably already aware of the influence of mental factors on sports performance – in learning, refining and maintaining skills, as well as in producing consistent high level performance. How often is a competition won by the performer who:

- handles pressure better
- is totally committed to a tough training regime
- maintains concentration in spite of distractions
- remains confident in the face of setbacks?

Think of occasions when you performed badly and decide why.

You can probably think of a number of occasions when you (or another performer) performed poorly because you did not believe in yourself (you lacked self-confidence), you became upset or frustrated by the weather conditions, an official's decisions made you angry, or you were distracted or psyched out by your opponent or perhaps the crowd. You may also be able to think of training or coaching sessions when your practice was poor; perhaps there was a lack of commitment and effort, your practice was purposeless and undirected – you were content to get through it rather than strive to maximise every opportunity and give 100% effort in terms of both physical application and mental attitude.

Most competitors use a variety of mental techniques to help them cope with difficult situations both in a sports context and perhaps in life more generally (eg dealing with examinations, interviews, work pressures, relationships). Often these strategies have been acquired as a result of experience or trial and error rather than through teaching. You can accelerate and enhance this process by systematically developing appropriate techniques for specific occasions. You may already use or be familiar with a number of techniques. Table 1 provides an overview of the type of skills that can be used to strengthen each quality.

Table 1: Overview of mental qualities and skills

Quality	Techniques/Strategies
Commitment	Goal-setting Refocusing Positive thinking (eg use of positive statements) Imagery
Concentration	Imagery Distraction training Developing routines and using crib cards segmenting performance into easy-to-manage components Simulated competition training
Control	Relaxation training Breathing exercises (eg centring) Cognitive restructuring Positive self-statements Developing routines Simulated competition training Imagery
Confidence	Positive self-talk/statements Imagery Goal-setting Routines Cognitive restructuring (positive thinking) Simulated competition training

You may have noticed that imagery appears under every quality. This demonstrates the versatility of imagery techniques and the way in which it can enhance all these qualities – but what exactly is imagery?

What is Imagery?

Imagery is referred to by various names. Some coaches and sports psychologists use the term **mental practice** to describe this process but this more accurately refers to the use of imagery to practise and condition technical skills. Another commonly used term, **visualisation,** is a particular type of mental rehearsal that emphasises only the visual sense to imagine a sport (or any other) situation. Imagery is best described as *a method of using all the senses to create or re-create an experience in the mind.* For most people, imagery represents creating pictures in the mind's eye of an event or task. However, as will become evident as you read through this booklet and try the exercises, imagery is this and much more.

Read how Steve Podborski, the former World Cup Downhill ski champion (cited in Orlick and Partington, 1986, p69) describes how imagery is used by elite skiers and why imagery is such a valuable technique.

'Another thing that gets you to the point where you are one of the elite, is the ability to visualise not only the way it looks when you are going down, but how it feels ... the muscle tension that you actually go through when you make the turns, and to experience what attitude your body is in ... I feel what things will feel like and see everything run through my head. I have a moving picture with feelings and sensations. When I'm doing these mental runs ... if I make a mistake, I'll stop the picture and back it up. Then I run through it and usually get it right the second time. I run through the entire course like that.'

Steve Podborski

At one time or another, most performers use their imagination – before, during or after competitions. Some daydream of illustrious successes – scoring the winning goal, achieving a personal best, winning the big race; others imagine dismal failure – falling off the beam, missing the critical putt. Your mind constantly creates visual pictures, experiences emotional occurrences and produces bodily sensations of sport experiences or movements whether you are wide awake or in deep sleep. Unfortunately, few coaches and performers have learnt how to maximise the daily use of imagery techniques to enhance training and performance.

Why is It Used?

Imagery can be used for a number of purposes. The most common include encouraging performers to:

- *see* successful performances (either rerun previous successes or seeing yourself or others successfully performing a new task)
- focus on the key factors which contribute to this success and develop strategies to enhance performance in similar situations in the future (ie improve consistency).

Each of these can contribute to enhanced performance. Mental imagery techniques are critical tools in most elite athletes' training regimes. Research[1] suggests that 85–90% of surveyed Olympic athletes regularly employ imagery rehearsal as a component of their training for competition.

In individual sports, such as golf and athletics, imagery has been used to programme the body for successful execution. The golfer, Jack Nicklaus, is well known for going to the movies in his head before every shot – to picture the target, see the flight path of the ball, watch it land and run on, and imagine himself using the correct swing for the shot. Dick Fosbury, the famous world class high jumper, often spent minutes imagining himself successfully jumping over the bar before beginning his run up. Steve Backley, the Olympic silver medallist in the javelin, uses imagery to practise his throws, which he describes as especially useful when injured or too fatigued to throw physically.

In team sports, imagery is used to assess opponent's strengths and weaknesses and to devise appropriate strategies and make decisions in order to succeed in a match. Superstar basketball player, Michael Jordan, says he visualises which moves and shots he will use against a specific opponent ahead of time so the right decisions are already made. The great rugby fly half, Rob Andrew, uses imagery to visualise the spots on the field where he will try to attack with his kicks. These examples further illustrate the versatility of imagery.

Why does it work? Your mind controls all your body movements. This mind-body connection occurs whether you actually execute a task or just think about executing one. In fact, your body does not know whether the controlling nervous impulses that move your muscles are generated through your imagination or your unconscious brain for purposeful movement.

---

1   Orlick and Partington, 1988.

Types of Imagery

Performers tend to use two distinct types of imagery, named on the basis of the senses involved and the visual perspective used. You are probably most familiar with **external** imagery, or the visual perspective you would experience watching your own body executing a skill (like watching yourself on a home video). For example, imagine a friend had videotaped you swinging a golf club and you were watching the playback of you hitting a drive off the first tee.

External perspective

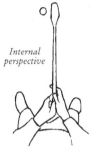

Internal perspective

Using an **internal** perspective, you would picture a visual image of the surroundings as if you were looking through your own eyes and simultaneously feeling the muscular contractions and movement sensations (kinesthetic feelings) that occur during actual movement. Using an internal perspective, the image would be much more vivid. Not only would you see everything happen – this time through your own eyes rather than those of the camera – you would also feel your hands on the club, the wind in your hair, your body rotate and the solid contact on impact as you swing. You might also hear the sound of the golf club during the swing and certainly at impact.

Stop to think when you might use internal and external imagery.

Performers tend to image from an external perspective when they are trying to correct errors or when first learning a sport skill – particularly if it is a closed task (ie ones that are self-paced and predominantly under the control of the performer such as a serve in tennis, taking a penalty in soccer or basketball). You might use an internal perspective to image well learnt movements or skills. Both perspectives are extremely useful and should be included in imagery programming. Table 2 describes the major benefits of each.

Table 2: Benefits of each type of imagery

Perspective	Benefits
External	• You can move your perspective around and so see the actions from various positions (not available to internal perspective) so you can analyse different aspects of the technique. • Can be used even if they have never executed the task before. • May be particularly helpful when learning a new skill (especially by demonstration) or when you are trying to isolate and correct mistakes in skill execution.
Internal	• More realistic experience of the actual movement, providing identical perceptual information – you see the surroundings as if they were actually there, you feel the movements as if executing the acts. • May offer more potential for performance benefits because it has the potential to use all the senses, and therefore it should aid the transfer of training to competition. • Can be rehearsed by performers to practise match strategies, rehearse recognition of visual and kinesthetic cues, identify and correct kinesthetic movement problems, cope with debilitating anxiety and rehabilitate injured body parts.

Some benefit is gained from switching perspective as required (see Exercise 6, page 38 which includes some tips on how to decide which perspective might be more beneficial for a specific sport situation and will also show you how to control the imagery perspective you wish to use).

How to Use It

To be effective, like any skill imagery needs to be developed and practised regularly. It will be most beneficial if certain principles are followed – it may help to think of the **4Rs:** relaxation, realism, regularity and reinforcement.

Relaxation means having a relaxed mind and body so you can become involved in the imagery exercises, feel your body moving and experience any emotions generated. The relaxation response seems to act like an eraser on the mind, wiping away the cares of the day so you can more easily concentrate on one thought at a time. It may help to use a relaxation technique[1] prior to imagery training (Exercise 2, page 29 incorporates some rhythmic breathing exercises to encourage relaxation).

Realism means creating imagery so realistic you believe you are actually executing the skill. You have probably heard the old expression *practice makes perfect.* A more precise statement is **perfect practice makes perfect.** In other words, you should practise the same way you want to play or perform. When you structure your training to mirror the actual competitive situation, you feel *as if you have been there before.* For example, if you are a basketball coach, you do not practise a last shot play for five seconds left in the game by taking ten seconds to execute the play. Or, if you are expected to perform before a large crowd, you might want to train in front of a noisy audience (or with an audiotape of a noisy crowd playing). In order to obtain the most realistic imagery possible, you must incorporate clarity, vividness, emotion, control and a positive outcome into your imagery:

- **Clarity** – most athletes do not image very clearly when they first start training. With proper practice, the vividness and control of images can be enhanced (Exercise 3, page 32).

- **Vividness** is the ability to incorporate as many of your senses as possible into your imagery so the scene is as clear and realistic as real life itself (ie experience the actions, physiological and emotional responses in your imagery as possible). You need to pay closer attention to your body movements and sensations when training and subsequently recall these verbally while practising imagery. For example, a crown or 10-pin bowler could practise a pendulum swing while standing on the approach or off the green to increase awareness of the sensations associated with the swing (Exercise 3, page 32).

- Try to include **emotional feelings** in your images. It may be necessary to refresh your memory constantly by emphasising specific sensory awareness (eg smell the grass) during training or to become familiar with specific competition sites by visiting venues beforehand, by videotaping the surroundings or by the description of someone who has competed there before (Exercise 7, page 40).

- Image **control** will also contribute to realism. Many of the exercises will help to improve imagery control – especially Exercises 4, 5 and 6.

---

1   The **sports coach UK** booklet *Handling Pressure* may be helpful. It is available from **Coachwise 1st4sport** (tel 0113-201 5555 or visit www.1st4sport.com).

'It took me a long time to control my images and perfect my imagery, maybe a year, doing it every day. At first I couldn't see myself, I always saw everyone else, or I would see my dives wrong all the time. I would get an image of hurting myself or tripping on the board, or I would *see* something done really bad. As I continued to work at it, I got to the point where I could see myself doing the perfect dive and the crowd yelling at the Olympics. But it took me a long time. I read everything I had to do and I knew my dive by heart. Then I started to see myself on the board doing my perfect dive. But some days I couldn't see it, or it was a bad dive in my head. I worked at it so much it got to the point that I could do all my dives easily.'

Orlick and Partington, 1988, p114

• Being able to image a positive **outcome** is also a crucial principle. If you think positively, you're more likely to succeed; if you think negatively, you are more likely to fail. Performers who visualise themselves missing the target or making a mistake in execution are more likely to do so in competition (Exercise 7, page 40).

Regularity suggests you must practise almost every day to gain the benefits of mental training. Like physical skills, mental skills must be practised regularly in order to transfer training effects to the competitive arena. Most research[1] indicates that for optimal effects you should spend three to five minutes of uninterrupted imagery concentration on each image scene. Too little time will result in poorly developed memory trace and inconsistent execution. Too much time spent on the same image will lead to boredom and fatigue, which will decrease concentration and subsequent performance. If you need to focus on one image for an extended period of time, intersperse your rehearsal with short rest periods.

---

1   For example, Murphy and Jowdy, 1992.

Gymnastics session to work on basic tumbling routine showing use of imagery

15 mins warm-up and stretching	Practise imaging the run up into the tumbling routine: the run up, hurdle step, lifting of the chest, the arm swing, flexion and rapid extension in the ankle, knee and hip joints.
40 mins on basic moves in tumbling routine	Watch self or others, imagine it externally, watch again, imagine internally; image cues – such as the position of the arm to initiate twist.

In rest periods between, watch video of previous attempt, image the routine, re-practise, video again focusing on the feel of the movement, image the feel.

Working on full routine   Externally watch, internally rehearse cues – such as arm position to initiate twisting moves, lifting of chest, position of head, controlling the landing.

Mental rehearsal should be a regular part of every training session and can even be used for a minimum 10–15 minutes a day outside training. To optimise mental rehearsal benefits, performers should alternate periods of actual physical practice with imagery practice. In fact, the best time to rehearse a skill mentally would be immediately after its successful execution. For example, a gymnast who has been practising a new move in her floor exercise routine should stop for a brief time immediately after she accomplished a successful move, and mentally replay the visual and kinesthetic aspects of the move. If immediate rehearsal is not possible, take several minutes to rehearse during water or training breaks, mentally rehearse in the changing room or at home. A number of exercises will help you to use imagery in training and then in competition (Exercises 9–14).

Reinforcement means using visual and kinesthetic aids to enhance the quality and control of your imagery. Most people have access to videotape cameras which can dramatically enhance imagery training ability. Performers often have hazy pictures of imagined skill components when they are first learning a skill, so seeing themselves perform an activity several times will more clearly imprint the image to memory. Visual aids can be particularly useful in instances where performers are experiencing recurrent errors in technique or form. Videotapes of their form taken from outside their perspective (external) can help to pinpoint continual problems so in their external imagery rehearsal, they can visualise correcting the errors and performing flawlessly. For instance, a tennis player was unaware that her elbow placement was poor during her service action. After several play-backs of mistakes and corrections on videotape with alternating imagery sessions, she was able to perfect successfully her serving motion. Exercise 9 (page 44) includes some ideas for using imagery to identify and correct errors.

4Rs – tips for success

1 It may help to use a **relaxation** technique prior to imagery training.

2 With practice, you can improve the vividness, control and feeling of **realism** of your imagery.

3 Frequent and **regular** practice within and outside training is needed to develop and maintain your imagery skills.

4 The quality and control of your imagery can be improved (**reinforcement**) by using video and kinesthetic aids.

Developing Imagery Skills

To comply with these principles and so maximise the effectiveness of imagery, there are certain training implications you need to adopt. The principles and implications are summarised in the table over the page and more detailed guidance on breaking down skills (segmenting) and slow motion to improve control is provided in the following text.

Table 3: Principles and training implications for developing imagery skills

Principle	Sub-principles	Training Implication	Exercise
Relaxation		Use relaxation skills prior to imagery training	2.1, 3.6
Realism	Clarity	Intersperse physical observation/practice with mental imagery practice to improve clarity	2.2, all ex 3 6.3
	Vividness	Encourage the use of as many senses as possible	all ex 3
	Emotion	Encouraging emotional content in imagery increases realism and so effectiveness. It also helps deal with the emotions of competition	7
	Control	Segment the skill – break it down into smaller components to visualise each part (eg in taking a basketball free throw: the pre-shot routine, the physical execution of the shot and the ball flight and drop through the ring)	all ex 4
		External and internal imagery are both valuable (eg external can be used to identify errors, internal offers greater realism and increases the transfer effect to competition)	3.7, 4.2 5.1 all ex 6
		Imaging in real time maximises the transfer effect to competition	all ex 5
		Slow motion imagery may be helpful but always finish the imagery session using the normal speed	5.2
	Positive outcome	Use negative imagery (eg to identify an error) very sparingly and always finish on a positive image	7.3
Regularity		3–5 minutes of uninterrupted imagery concentration seems to be most effective	9
		Mental imagery should be a regular part of every training session and a minimum 10–15 minutes a day outside training should be encouraged	3.6, 9.1, 10.1
Reinforcement		Use visual and kinesthetic aids (eg video) to enhance the effectiveness of imagery	3.7
		The writing of imagery scripts may help you plan the content and timing of your sessions and so maximise the effects on learning and performance	8.1, 11.1, 13.1, 14.1

To control the image and so the outcome of the action, it may help to break down the skill in the imagery exercise into small components (**segmenting**) so you can visualise each part successfully. For example, there is a classic story of the basketball player using imagery prior to taking a penalty from the free throw line; he would bounce the ball but could not image it returning from the floor. By breaking down the skill into three components (pre-shot routine, act of shooting and ball swishing through the hoop), and practising imaging each part separately, he was eventually able to put them together in a fluid progression (Exercise 4.1, page 35).

You can also try to use **slow motion** imagery for each component to help you see each part clearly. This imagery technique can be particularly useful when first learning a skill. Slow motion replays of a task can give you a clearer picture of the task progression. For example, players learning the proper technique for a quick shot in ice or field hockey might benefit from seeing the action slowed down to get a vivid image of the timing and the sequencing of body parts. They could then mentally rehearse at this slower speed to commit the order and mechanics of each component to memory (Exercise 5.2, page 37).

Slow motion imagery can also be helpful in high speed skills that are completed in a second or two (eg diving, high jumping, gymnastics). The important bodily cues or components, like a particular arm position on a dive or leg position in the high jump, can be easily identified and practised through the method of slow motion imagery. You may find slow motion imagery difficult at first but this can be improved with practice (Exercise 5, page 37 will help). However, remember as the normal execution is at real speed, you cannot transfer the maximum benefits from training to competition by over-emphasising slow motion imagery in training.

Effective imagery training sessions do not happen by accident. Just like the fitness and skill based aspects of your training sessions, you must carefully plan the content and timing of your imagery exercises and rehearsal to maximise effects on learning and performance. To do this, you may need to write your own individualised **imagery scripts** to be used for a particular training purpose (Exercise 8, page 42).

> **NB: Always end your imagery sessions with normal speed imagery so your mental rehearsal speed matches your physical competition speed and, therefore, maximises the transfer of training.**

Writing scripts is just like writing a short story; simply follow the three steps.

1   Telling the basic story

Outline the basic content of the act or situation to be imagined – write it in the first person (I) if you are using it yourself or the second person (you), if it is to be read to someone else. To describe a skill execution, make sure you include all **components** of the skill to be imagined or **behaviours** to be emphasised, especially if it is a complex skill. If you are describing the events in a sport situation, include all actions that occur in the event and the correct sequencing of all the actions.

> ### Examples of tennis serve
>
> #### 1   Telling the basic story
> Components:
>
> - Preparation
> - Ball toss
> - Impact
> - Recovery
> - Ball flights and landing in service box

2   Adding the details

Add the **sensory stimuli** – the descriptors (adjectives) that add colour, detail (eg context, weather) and movement qualities (eg speed of movement) to the original script components or events.

Add the movement or **kinesthetic** feelings, physiological or body responses, and the emotional responses. The words that are added are action words such as verbs and adverbs that clearly describe the quality of actions or emotions.

> #### 2   Adding the details
> Seeing the racket in the hand, the bright yellow ball rebounding against the green court as you bounce it in preparation, seeing the position of the opponent, looking at the point on the court where you will direct the serve.
>
> Feeling the relaxed shoulders and hands, the racket grip in the hand, seeing the bright yellow ball nestled on the fingers in the hand, feeling the smooth release of the ball at the arm's full stretch, feeling the body weight shift, the knees bend, the body rising upward as the knees extend, feeling the power in the body, the racket head accelerate, the wrist snap, the sound of the racket making contact with the ball, watching the ball swerve and land in the centre corner of the green service box and kick away for a clean ace. Feel the exhilaration and pleasure.

3   Refining the script

You will want to rewrite the components or actions into a paragraph that can be read easily and clearly. Read it to yourself and try to imagine the event in all its sensory, action and emotional detail. Do you feel as if you are actually executing the skill or experiencing the event? If not, re-examine the descriptors and action words to see if they accurately reflect the sensations associated with this action.

> #### 3   Refining the script
> Rewrite the script until when you read it, you feel as if you are executing the serve.

If it works, you might choose to put it onto audiotape so you can use it regularly as a prompt for your imagery rehearsal sessions and use it effectively in training sessions or competition.

When to do Imagery Training

Imagery has many potential uses in training and competition. Most imagery training programmes work through the following progressions (highlighted in Figure 1):

1   Start with introductory educational sessions about imagery, imagery ability assessment, imagery rehearsal of basic sport skills and relaxation imagery (Exercises 1–3).

2   Progress to exercises to develop clarity and control based on the principles of the 4Rs (Exercises 4–7).

3   Employ imagery for skill development and maintenance (Exercise 9, page 44) and to strengthen the particular qualities (eg the 4Cs) needed for high performance (Exercises 10–14).

4   Practise imagery for use in specific situations – such as immediately before the event, after breaks in action, at critical points such as when taking a penalty, after a mistake (Exercise 17, page 54). These images would include repeated rehearsal of simple and complex skills, competitive strategies, and enhancement of other psychological skills by incorporating imagery rehearsal into training (Exercises 9–17).

5   Once you have developed good basic imagery skills, you should practise imagery-based interventions before competitions that include pre-competitive and competitive routines to use prior to, during and after actual competition (Exercise 18, page 55). As the season progresses and more important competitions occur, you can revise imagery scripts to meet the special pressures and requirements of elite competitions.

6   Even in the off-season, you can use imagery training to begin programming yourself toward certain goals in the next season. You can read more about mental skills training and begin to practise imagery techniques out of training. Remember, imagery does not require equipment nor does it lead to fatigue. Finally, you can begin thinking about additions or improvements to skills that you wish to undertake in the next season (Exercise 16, page 53).

1	2	3	4	5	6
Introductory sessions to introduce imagery	Exercise to develop clarity and control	For skill development & to strengthen qualities	For specific & critical situations	Before, during & after competition	In the off-season

Figure 1: Introducing, developing and integrating imagery skills

When to Use Imagery

When do you use it? When might you use it?

Think about your current use of imagery:

- How frequently do you use it?
- How effectively?
- How vividly?
- Can you control it?
- When do you use it?

Imagery training and interventions can be used for a number of purposes in sport:

To enhance physical skills
This involves using imagery rehearsal for remembering movement feelings, practising perfect execution and correcting errors (Exercise 9, page 44).

To enhance perceptual skills
This includes mentally learning and rehearsing sport strategies for cue focus, decision-making or problem-solving activities (Exercise 10, page 46).

To enhance psychological skills
These might include learning to control over-arousal and anxiety before and during competition, programming goals into your mind, creating more self-confidence and self-efficacy through mastery images and self-talk, focusing and refocusing attention during performance through routines and plans, and speeding injury recovery and overcoming mental blocks resulting from injury. The remainder of this section looks at this area in more detail.

Imagery for commitment. Commitment involves developing motivational skills that encourage performers to set competitive goals and regularly train to improve and persist in activities even when immediate progress is not apparent. It has been described by some as the will to win, mental toughness or the tenacity to persist when the going is tough. Without commitment, no challenging long-term goals can be achieved and performance enhancement remains a dream. Athletes must accept goals as their own and put in the regular effort that brings improvement and success.

Imagery training can be an important tool in maintaining commitment toward sporting achievements. Performers can learn to incorporate images of achievements and goals into their training and competition routines. Examples might include imaging a specific time, distance or score in a race or event, a top three finish in a race, perfect execution of a task, achieving a specific target behaviour that is a short-term goal step toward a long-term goal, or just visually seeing the goal written out in their mind's eye. These goal programming images can be regularly rehearsed in training, immediately before a competitive event, or out of training to maintain commitment (Exercise 11, page 47).

Imagery for concentration. Concentration involves being able to maintain an appropriate focus during training and competition to ensure you are paying attention to important task cues and responding correctly and quickly. Athletes must be able to switch attentional focus during competition to broad and narrow foci and externally on the environmental cues or internally on thoughts and strategies. Like other mental skills, you need to practise regularly attending to various cues during training to ensure you are maintaining the proper focus during the high anxiety and complexity of the competitive setting[1]. Your goal should be to have rehearsed the cues many times so cue identification and processing in competition becomes an automatic process that does not take a lot of time and effort to occur.

Several types of mental images can be used during training and competition to reach this goal of maintaining focus and automatically processing performance cues. For example, imagery cue words or triggers can be rehearsed when learning and performing different skill components (eg *smooth* golf swing, *kick through the spot* in kicking sports, *knees, toes and in* for basketball free throw shooting). Or athletes can practise competitive images of reading cues for decision-making (eg a soccer or basketball player quickly assessing the opponent's defensive positions and team-mate's offensive positions to decide whether to dribble, pass or shoot). At certain instances in competition, it may be necessary to focus attention on details in the environment (eg the pebbly feel of a basketball, the firm grip on a racket) or yourself (eg muscle tension in one part of the body or heart rate). Finally, many endurance athletes practise images to cope with the pain of exertion or minor injuries when competing in a high intensity race (eg focusing on positive thoughts or the finish line during the pain of the final kick or sprint for home).

---

1   For further help, you are recommended to refer to the **sports coach UK** resource, *Improving Concentration*, available from **Coachwise 1st4sport** (tel 0113-201 5555 or visit www.1st4sport.com).

Imagery can be used to rehearse focusing and refocusing plans so you can remain on task during the stress of competition and return to the proper task cues for success if you have a prior mistake or unexpected event occur. For example, Orlick (1986) tells of an Olympic slalom canoeist who devised a plan that included cue words (eg *power, smooth, push*) to maintain focus during different segments of a race. He also asked athletes to rehearse mentally a Plan B in case Plan A was not working or in case an unexpected potential distraction occurred before or during an event (eg equipment breaks, delay in start, mistake in early part of event). Since the goal is to maintain concentration and not to become ruffled by distractions, competitors can rehearse focusing and refocusing plans to reduce uncertainty about the competitive environment and allow them to refocus when irregular events occur. The final goal is adapting to whatever occurs with minimal disruption to performance. If you have mentally prepared for the unexpected, you are more likely to adapt quickly and maintain high level performance (Exercise 12, page 48).

Imagery for confidence. Self-confidence occurs when you believe you can be successful and competent. It is enhanced by having been successful in executing a skill or at an event in the past, imagining yourself or others successfully completing the task, or by verbally persuading yourself you can successfully accomplish the skill. If you believe you can succeed in your mind, you have a better chance of succeeding in actual competition.

Mental imagery can be particularly powerful in creating self-confidence. You can learn to replay successful performances in your imagination so you feel positive about your ability to succeed. In addition, just observing another athlete or coach successfully demonstrate the proper execution of a skill can enhance self-confidence if you then imagine yourself achieving success on the same skill. Finally, you can add positive self-talk and affirmations into your images to enhance the effect by practising verbal persuasion on yourself while you imagine correct performance and then using the same statements during competition[1].

1   For further help, you are recommended to refer to the **sports coach UK** resource, *Building Self-confidence*, available from **Coachwise 1st4sport** (tel 0113-201 5555 or visit www.1st4sport.com).

There is some evidence to suggest that coping imagery may have a greater effect on feelings of self-confidence than mastery images. **Mastery** images involve imagining the perfect execution of a skill, while **coping** images involve imagining you have overcome an obstacle or difficulty during performance and finally succeeding in the task. Since the latter example is closer to reality, it is advisable to use coping images first but always finish with mastery, a perfect execution (Exercise 13, page 49).

Imagery for control. Some athletes need to modify their arousal level or reduce anxiety prior to or during competition[1]. Imagery can be an important part of stress management for you in tense situations which can teach you to control your bodily responses and worries resulting from competitive anxiety. Relaxing images of warm, safe place (eg lying on a warm beach) can help you deal with stress. With coping images, you can imagine taking deep breaths or feeling relaxed and then going on to perform successfully. As with confidence images, positive affirmations about your ability to cope with, for example, the crowd, noise or competition can also be included in **coping** images. Some athletes in more anaerobically-based events like sprinting and weight-lifting may need to psych-up to a higher level for one effort. These performers can imagine being quick or 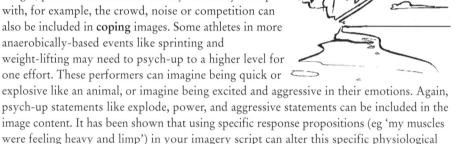 explosive like an animal, or imagine being excited and aggressive in their emotions. Again, psych-up statements like explode, power, and aggressive statements can be included in the image content. It has been shown that using specific response propositions (eg 'my muscles were feeling heavy and limp') in your imagery script can alter this specific physiological response (Exercise 14, page 50).

To enhance performance in competition

Anecdotal evidence (Orlick, 1986, 1990; Orlick and Partington, 1988) has shown that successful elite athletes practise and use pre-competitive and competitive routines as a way of coping with competitive stress and the uncertainty of competition. Imagery rehearsal is a large part of these routines where athletes imagine success, coping with anxiety or rehearsing strategies to try to ensure they will perform consistently and positively. These routines help athletes to remain focused, deal with distractions, cope with the panic of a mistake or poor start, and feel confident in their abilities. A number of critical moments can be identified when imagery-based routines might be used (based on work by Hardy and Fazey, 1990).

---

1   For further help, you are recommended to refer to the **sports coach UK** resource, *Handling Pressure,* available from **Coachwise 1st4sport** (tel 0113-201 5555 or visit www.1st4sport.com).

Table 4: Possible use of imagery at critical moments

When	Critical Moment	Purpose
Before, during and after training	Performance rehearsal	To rehearse skill learning and performance
Before competition	Instant preview	Relaxing images, repetition of simple and advanced skills, competitive strategies, past successes, goal programming
During competition	Preview during performance	For example of actual skill execution, strategies and plays; to rehearse actual movement and events prior to them occurring
During competition	Instant review	Rehearse the feeling of a movement or play after successful execution to commit to memory; or to identify and rectify an error
After competition	Performance review	To evaluate good and bad aspects of performance after competition to assist training planning and reward good play

Pre-competition routine (instant preview). Orlick (1990) describes the pre-race routine of an athletics sprinter who uses imagery and rehearsed cue words to imagine success in the race and feeling the way he wants to run the race (eg *explode* out of the blocks, *float* as you run fluidly). Jack Nicklaus is famous for his use of imagery on a pre-shot routine. He sees the ball land where he wants it to land, imagines the flight of the ball, and imagines the smooth swing before he steps up to the ball. Often in the Winter Olympics or during ski season, television shows downhill racers or slalom skiers visualising the course during warm-up at the ski hut before the start. During competition, you often see high jumpers (the American, Dwight Stones, is a good example) imagine themselves successfully jumping over the bar before beginning the run-up. The Welsh rugby goal kicker, Neil Jenkins, can be seen imagining the ball clearing the bar between the posts and goes through the motions of kicking before he begins his approach.

Most elite athletes develop imagery-based routines to help them reap the benefits of training on competition day. Once appropriate images have been identified and scripts written, these image-based routines must be practised repeatedly in training simulations and friendlies before they are used with confidence in major competitions.

During-competition routines. In addition to using routines prior to the start of a competition, many sports have natural breaks in the competition which allow performers time to use imagery to maintain focus, improve confidence and rehearse strategies. These breaks might include time-outs, half times, dead ball situations, during an injury, after a goal is scored and at a penalty. They provide athletes with the opportunity to use imagery-based routines (**preview during performance**) to enhance performance and maintain control. You can also build scripts and routines to cope with replaying skills or strategies after its completion (**instant review**) – either to reinforce the correct movement or to identify the error and then rehearse the correct movement.

Post-competition review. Performance review allows you to replay good and poor parts of the competition to identify areas for future training, correct mistakes and build self-confidence for the future. You need to develop and use a post-competitive routine to do this. You might develop the habit of doing this at a specific time – for example in the shower, on the way home, before going to sleep at night. Good portions of performance should be rehearsed so you feel proud of your accomplishments and build self-confidence. Mistakes should be mentally rehearsed to identify where they occurred in execution and then the perfect execution should be rehearsed – always finish with the correct execution.

Summary

Imagery techniques can be used both within and outside training and before, during and after competition. Perhaps the greatest advantage is its ease of application. You can use mental rehearsal almost anywhere (eg in the changing room, before going to bed, between points), in a short amount of time (once proficient, in seconds) and for long periods with minimal physical fatigue (although short sessions are probably better). The key to effective mental imagery practice is to learn how to rehearse mentally to maximise your potential, and then like any physical skill, follow a daily training routine. In the next sections, you will have an opportunity to put some of these principles into action by selecting and working through exercises.

SECTION TWO
Exercises to Improve your Imagery Skills

Introduction

In this section, you will find eight imagery exercises designed to help you develop your skills. If you have little or no experience, you may want to work progressively through the exercises in the order they are written. If however, you are looking to hone your skills and seek greater help in how to use them in competitive situations, you may wish to skip the first set of exercises.

EXERCISE 1
ASSESSING YOUR IMAGERY SKILLS

Many people already imagine and daydream. To choose the most helpful exercises for you, first assess your own imagery skills.

If you already use imagery quite regularly with some success, work through the exercises under A; if you use it rarely, select the exercises in B and if you have limited or no knowledge, try the exercise in C.

A.I

If you already use imagery, profile[1] your own imagery skills to determine your strengths and weaknesses and so select the sort of exercises to help you develop and apply your skills in training and competition. Think of all the qualities and aspects of imagery – for example internal, external, relaxed, clarity, control, speed, duration, outcome, perspective, emotions, use of various senses. Then write what you perceive to be the most important qualities on the perimeter of the blank profiling chart on the opposite page. Use the example profile in Figure 2 as a guide if helpful. Alternatively, you may wish to use the **Assessment and Monitoring Form** provided in Appendix B (page 60).

---

1 For further information on profiling, you are recommended to refer to the **sports coach UK** resource and audiotape, *Performance Profiling*, available from **Coachwise 1st4sport** (tel 0113-201 5555 or visit www.1st4sport.com).

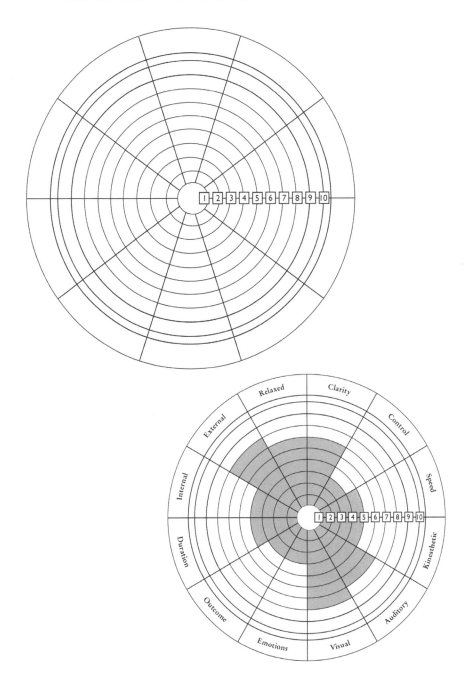

Figure 2: Sample profile of imagery strengths and weaknesses of a male basketball player

Rate the importance on a scale of 1 to 10 of each quality – remember, different aspects of performance place different demands on imagery use. Then rate yourself on a scale of one to ten on each one by marking the segment. On the basketball player example, notice he rates himself as much stronger on external than internal, with better visual and auditory than kinesthetic imagery. There is a relative weakness in his ability to control the imagery, its duration, accuracy of speed and outcome, as well as some difficulty in generating strong emotional content.

Look at the greatest areas of discrepancy and/or relative weakness and determine the aspect/s of imagery most critical to the particular elements of performance you want to rehearse. Set yourself an action plan and time-scale for improvement, then select appropriate exercises to meet your training needs. The basketball player, for example, might have written an action plan to improve his kinesthetic imagery skills or perhaps his ability to control his imagery.

<table>
<tr><td>

Action plan for basketball player

Priority areas:
Improve my kinesthetic rating from 5 to 7

Process goal:
Spend ten minutes every day in the shower working on my kinesthetic imagery exercises

Selected exercises:
Appropriate exercises from 2 and 3

Time frame for implementation/ reassessment on:
Four weeks today (17 July 1998)

</td><td>

Your action plan

Priority areas:

Process goal:

Selected exercises:

Time frame for implementation/ reassessment on:

</td></tr>
</table>

A.II

You may also wish to profile your ability to use imagery in different situations. Using the same ten-point scale, rate your current and ideal scores for each of the imagery uses on the following chart[1]. Add other situations if appropriate:

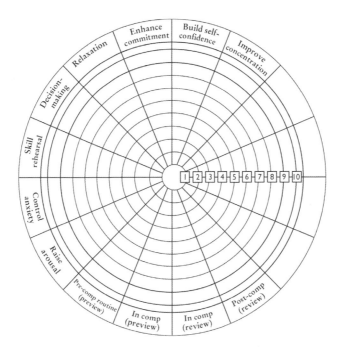

Look at the differences between ideal and current scores on each profile and prioritise the area/s in which you feel an improvement would make a significant difference to your ability to use imagery in training and competition.

Write an action plan using process goals (to improve score by x), selecting relevant exercises from this pack or other books to show how and when you will develop your imagery skills:

1   You may wish to photocopy this first for multiple use.

Action plan
Priority areas:

Process goal:

Selected exercises:

Time frame for implementation/reassessment on:

A similar assessment and monitoring form can be found for photocopying for regular use in Appendix B (page 60).

B

If you use very little imagery, try to establish when (situation), why (purpose) and how (type) you use it or might use it, and how effectively (use the same ten-point rating scale).

Situation	Purpose	Type	Effectiveness

Set yourself an action plan and timescale for improvement, then select appropriate exercises to meet your training needs.

Action plan
Priority areas:

Process goal:

Selected exercises:

Time frame for implementation/reassessment on:

C If you do not use imagery and have limited or no knowledge, do the following exercise and then assess your skills using the evaluation questions provided.

Sit down in a quiet place without distractions and where you are unlikely to be disturbed. Either read the following script for yourself and stop after each sentence, shut your eyes and focus on the imagery OR ask someone to read the script for you while you create the images.

Imagine yourself picking up an orange from a fruit bowl. Note the colours of the rest of the fruit in the bowl – the yellow of the bananas, the green and red of the apples, the black of the grapes and the orange of the oranges and satsumas.

Feel the surface of the orange in your fingers and note its smell.

See the zest spring from the orange as you dig your fingernails into the skin.

Be aware of the smell of the orange, as you continue to peel the skin away.

Note the noise as you peel the orange and split it into segments.

Feel the sticky zest and juice on your fingers.

Experience the taste of the orange and the feel of it in your mouth and on your teeth as you bite into a segments and chew it.

Then answer the following questions.

How easily were you able
to create the images?   *very easily / easily / a little / hardly at all / not at all*

Which sense did you find easiest ?   *sight / sound / smell / touch / taste*

Which did you find most difficult?   *sight / sound / smell / touch / taste*

Did you use internal or external imagery?   *internal / external / mixture*

How often do you use some form
of imagery in your sport?   *very often / often / sometimes / hardly ever / never*

How useful do you think imagery could
be to your sports performance?   *extremely / very / somewhat / a little / not at all*

Set yourself an action plan and timescale for improvement, then select appropriate
exercises to meet your training needs.

Action plan
Priority areas:

Process goal:

Selected exercises:

Time frame for implementation/reassessment on:

EXERCISE 2
INTRODUCING IMAGERY

Some people are readily able to create vivid images in their mind; others need more practice and guidance.

2.1

First read the following instructions for an imagery-based relaxation session and then choose a quiet place and comfortable position to work through them practically. It may help to ask someone to read the instructions to you while you carry out the exercise. The text should be read quite slowly, allowing ample time between each paragraph for you to create the images.

Lie down and relax your entire body. If you hear noises, don't try to block them out but focus on your breathing – inhaling, then exhaling slowly.

Once you have established an effective breathing pattern, focus your attention on an image or situation you find particularly tranquil – perhaps a gentle waterfall, rolling hills, a beautiful sunset, a sunny beach. Try to create a vivid image – see the shapes, colours, textures, people – all in as much detail as possible.

Note any sounds – perhaps of water, birds, voices. Notice any smells – of the sea air, sun cream, flowers. Try to feel any sensations – the breeze on your face, the wind in your hair, the sand between your toes, the water on your feet. Are there any tastes – the salt air, ice cream, a cool drink?

Don't worry if you find yourself wandering from one image to another – it is useful to experiment to find the ideal image that elicits the most relaxed response. Continue this exercise until you are easily able to hold the images effortlessly.

When you wish to return to a higher level of consciousness, count upwards from one to seven, counting on each exhalation, gradually experiencing greater alertness and awareness of the external environment. When you reach seven, you should feel fully awake, relaxed and refreshed.

After the session, rate in your logbook how well you were able to carry out the exercise, using appropriate scales on the form over the page.

Name:		Date:
Time:	Place:	

Attribute	Rating scale			Comments
Level of relaxation	very uptight	somewhat relaxed	perfectly relaxed	
	1 2 3	4 5 6 7 8	9 10	
Visual content	can't see anything	somewhat vivid and accurate	perfectly accurate	
	1 2 3	4 5 6 7 8	9 10	
Auditory content	can't hear anything	somewhat vivid and accurate	perfectly accurate	
	1 2 3	4 5 6 7 8	9 10	
Touch content	can't feel anything	somewhat vivid and accurate	perfectly accurate	
	1 2 3	4 5 6 7 8	9 10	
Kinesthetic content	can't feel anything	somewhat vivid and accurate	perfectly accurate	
	1 2 3	4 5 6 7 8	9 10	
Smell content	can't smell anything	somewhat vivid and accurate	perfectly accurate	
	1 2 3	4 5 6 7 8	9 10	
Taste content	can't taste anything	somewhat vivid and accurate	perfectly accurate	
	1 2 3	4 5 6 7 8	9 10	
General sensory content	no sensory images	somewhat vivid and accurate	perfectly accurate	
	1 2 3	4 5 6 7 8	9 10	
Internal control	no internal control	some control	perfect control	
	1 2 3	4 5 6 7 8	9 10	
External control	no external control	some control	perfect control	
	1 2 3	4 5 6 7 8	9 10	
Emotional content	no emotion	some emotion	perfect emotion	
	1 2 3	4 5 6 7 8	9 10	
Effectiveness of script	not effective	somewhat effective	perfectly effective	
	1 2 3	4 5 6 7 8	9 10	

Evaluation form

A copy of the form for photocopying can be found in Appendix C (page 62).

2.2

Select a basic skill from your sport (eg scoring a goal or a shot, making a successful pass to a team-mate, executing a gymnastics move flawlessly). Read (or ask someone to read to you) the following directions and try the mental rehearsal exercises. Remember you will find the imagery exercises much easier if you choose a quiet place where you will not be disturbed, a comfortable position and start by gaining a relaxed state.

Imagine you are inside your body and about to picture yourself executing (a particular skill) successfully. Try to visualise from an internal perspective (ie through your own eyes), feel the kinesthetic sensations of your movements, experience as many senses as you can and notice any emotions that result. Imagine what it feels like to perform the skill perfectly and see the successful end result (eg ball going in, high score given, team-mate taking the pass and scoring).

Try the exercise twice and then assess how well you were able to do this using appropriate scales on a copy of the Evaluation Form in Appendix C (page 62).

NB: 3–5 minutes of uninterupted imagery concentration seems to be most effective.

EXERCISE 3
IMPROVING IMAGE INTENSITY (CLARITY/ VIVIDNESS)

Imagery is most effective when the greatest number of senses are evoked and the images are as vivid and potent as possible.

3.1

In a warm and relaxed environment, select a piece of sports equipment (eg the ball, stick, glove, clothing) and closely examine it, carefully noting the details – such as colours, designs, insignias, company logos and shape. With closed eyes, imagine the object in all its intricate colours, designs, exact shape. Open your eyes and rate the experience on a scale of 1–5 for visual imagery ability.

Can't see anything		Somewhat vivid and accurate		Perfectly vivid
1	2	3	4	5

Repeat the experience several times, each time observing the object, then trying to recreate it in your mind in the greatest possible detail, and assessing the effectiveness of the visual imagery.

> **NB: It can be useful to reintroduce the object stimulus to improve the clarity of the visual imagery. Alternate between visually examining the object and imagining it for several repetitions. Just like in sport, correct, repetitive practice will lead to improved imagery ability.**

3.2

Pick up the piece of equipment again and this time focus on the feel and texture of the material; search for differences in the texture or temperature. Close your eyes as you carefully handle the equipment. Put down the equipment and try to remember what it feels like to the touch. Try it several times, alternating between feeling the object and then trying to recreate the feel in your mind. Once again, rate the potency of the imagery using the five point scale:

Can't feel anything		Somewhat vivid and accurate		Perfectly vivid
1	2	3	4	5

Sometimes by blocking your predominant sense, vision, you can enhance your imagery ability. If it is a safe skill you are practising or you have time to step back and closely examine the sporting scene, then closing your eyes and using only your other senses can improve less used imagery senses such as **tactile imagery.**

3.3

Close your eyes and try to visualise the training environment – first the sights – the walls, floor, ceiling, lighting, equipment, markings if it is an internal venue; the ground, the markings, the sky, trees, equipment and so on if is outside. Try to visualise some of the people – ground staff, managers, performers – and start to see the training session about to take place. Next, try to hear the sounds that typify the training scene – traffic, other users, sound of the people training or practising. Focus on the sounds. Afterwards rate how well you were able to recapture these:

Can't hear anything		Somewhat vivid and accurate		Perfectly vivid
1	2	3	4	5

3.4

Choose a relatively simple skill to try to practise kinesthetic imagery. For example, in tennis the service toss might be ideal; in athletics, the first step of a sprint start; in football, a simple pass with the inside of your foot. Take up the proper position and execute the movement physically several times (with or without the actual ball or implement).

Now close your eyes and execute the movement in your mind. Focus on the kinesthetic feelings in the critical parts of your body executing the skill. Experience it from inside your body (ie use internal imagery rather than external – through the eye of a camera), look where you normally look during the action, and feel how your body moves. Repeat this several times. Again, afterwards rate how well you were able to recapture the feel of the movement using the five point scale:

Can't feel my body		Somewhat vivid and accurate		Perfectly vivid
1	2	3	4	5

By closing your eyes and focusing attention on critical body parts during movement, you will help to improve kinesthetic ability. Skilled athletes who have executed a movement many times are usually very good at kinesthetic imagery.

3.5

Watch an expert execute a simple skill and focus on one or two specific components of the action (eg in tennis, the ball toss and racket head; in swimming, the elbow lift and hand as it enters the water). Close your eyes and imagine what this skill component clearly looks like in all its reality. Try it several times and then physically practise the action several times (without the ball, without entering the water). Focus first on the visual action, then the feel of the movement. Close your eyes and focus on the movement sensations as you try the action physically. Once you can feel the kinesthetic sensations of the action, close your eyes and imagine seeing the movement through your own eyes and feeling the sensations of the movement. Imagine this several times to enhance the clarity of your visual imagery and kinesthetic (movement) imagery. Always record and evaluate the effectiveness each time you use imagery.

3.6

A relaxed state improves the intensity and clarity of the image. At your next warm-up before training, try a simple relaxation technique and practise using imagery to prepare to execute the skills you will be using later.

As you start the stretching routine, take several deep breaths from your stomach, totally filling your lungs with air and then slowly exhaling to remove all air. As you exhale, let the muscles sag and become limp. As you continue breathing deeply from your stomach, imagine a simple skill in your sport. Try to see how the skill looks (external perspective) and then image it from inside your moving body and imagine how the movement feels. Image the skill several times as you stretch and breathe deeply.

Always record and evaluate the effectiveness each time you use imagery.

> **NB: Visual aids such as competent demonstrations, emphasised visual cues, film loops, videotape recorders, hand-held mini cameras, videotape analysis systems, and even high-tech biomechanics analysis systems can be useful teaching aids to enhance the clarity and control of imagery pictures.**
> **Similarly, kinesthetic aids, such as weighted sports implements, performance aids (eg gymnastics harnesses), internal perspective video analysis, biofeedback systems, and in future, virtual reality imaging systems, can all help you develop proper kinesthetic awareness of sports movements and the ability to imagine using a kinesthetic emphasis.**

3.7

Try to use an imagery exercise in your next training session and make use of a visual or kinesthetic imagery aid or both. For example, you might ask someone to video your practice session so you can first watch yourself execute a particular technique, then shut your eyes and image yourself. This can help you develop your external imagery skills.

You may have to be a little more innovative to use video to help your internal imagery for it needs to replicate how you see things through your own eyes. There are many occasions where television crews now use this for special effects – the camera placed on the skis of the downhill skier, on the dashboard of the racing car, on the pedal of the cyclist, in the cricket stump. It need not be as sophisticated – for example for the golfer, you might shoot over the shoulder to look down the fairway to judge the direction, down at his/her feet to see his/her foot alignment and the ball. You can then carry out the same exercise, alternating watching the video, then shutting your eyes and trying to see and feel the movement. Always record and evaluate the effectiveness each time you use imagery.

EXERCISE 4

IMPROVING CLARITY AND CONTROL

You need to be able to control the image – to create perfect and vivid images with a positive outcome.

4.1

Select a skill, technique or component of a sporting action (eg a tennis serve, a gymnastics vault) and observe an expert demonstration model (eg through video, an accomplished performer), close your eyes and imagine the technique several times. Break the action down and practise physically a segment of the action – for example the run-up in a vault, the release of the ball onto the backboard in the lay-up in basketball. Focus on what you see, close your eyes and focus on the movement sensation (eg the feel of the knee lift in the run-up, the wrist action in the shot).

Once you can feel the kinesthetic sensations of the demonstrated action, close your eyes and imagine seeing the movement through your own eyes and feeling the sensations of the movement. Do this several times. Gradually do this for each component of the skill, repeating it until clarity is high when you should move on to the next component. Build up using the various components of the action, working through the stages of observation of demonstration, physical practice and visualisation with closed eyes.

Next observe a demonstration of the whole action and try to visualise the whole sequence of movements several times. If you have difficulty with the whole technique, repeat the visualisation of the components and, if necessary, repeat the demonstration to assist in creating an appropriate image.

Once you can perform this successfully, rehearse physically the various components sequentially with eyes first open and then closed. Do this for each component in sequence, until you can physically perform the whole skill and can successfully imagine visualising and feeling the movements of the whole skill.

NB: A video playback can help to provide the repeated demonstrations of the action. Scientific evidence[1] clearly shows that imagery used correctly with physical practice can speed up motor skill learning and aid performance of well learned skills. Remember to use the three stages: the observation, physical practice and then the imagery.

Now try to visualise from an internal viewpoint and feel the movements of the technique.

1   Murphy and Jowdy, 1992.

4.2

To develop a more powerful visual aid to internal visualisation, try to video from an internal perspective. With a hand-held camera, film as you go through the execution of the task to record the same cues you would normally see (eg the football player kicking at goal would see the keeper or posts and focus on the spot where the ball was to be kicked). This videotaped internal perspective helps the generation of the kinesthetic feelings that accompany the movement. Once you have viewed this internal tape several times, shut your eyes and imagine the same perspective and feel the sensations of movement more easily.

Always record and evaluate the effectiveness each time you use imagery.

EXERCISE 5

IMPROVING INTERNAL IMAGERY BY CONTROLLING SPEED AND DURATION

To maximise transfer to the competitive situation, learn to imagine sport skills and situations at their real life speed. Use slow motion imagery to analyse skill execution to identify and correct movements.

5.1 To improve internal imagery by controlling speed and duration, select a basic technique you practise regularly in training – choose a fairly closed and discrete skill (ie one that has a clear beginning and end, and can be executed without too much influence from outside factors). Using a stopwatch and a helper, time accurately how long it takes you to execute the technique – you'll have to agree what constitutes the start and completion. Do this at least twice and note the average time.

Now imagine executing the task as you have just performed it – from an internal perspective, through your own eyes and feeling the movements. Close your eyes, start the stopwatch as you begin imaging the action, and stop the watch when you have completed it. Compare the time it takes you to execute the technique physically with the time to execute it in your imagination.

If the imaged task was too fast, try it again and focus on and add more components to the execution (if appropriate) or slow down the imagery speed. If it is too slow, speed up the imagery processing and reduce the time spent on various components (remember: the aim is to reproduce a natural timing). With several repetitions of this exercise, you should be able to approximate closely the imagery time to the actual execution time. Always record and evaluate the effectiveness each time you use imagery.

5.2 Using a video camera and playback system, video a basic technique from start to finish. Play it back in slow motion so you can clearly see the various components and time the duration on a stopwatch. Close your eyes and try to visualise the same technique in slow motion. Ask someone to time your imagery on the stopwatch – starting it when you indicate with your hand that you are beginning the imagery and stopping it when you give the hand signal that you have completed the slow motion imagery of the technique. Check the corresponding times. Alternate watching the slow motion video replay and practising the slow motion imagery until the times are approximately the same. Finish the exercise by playing the videotape at normal speed and then visualising at normal speed. Again compare the times for normal execution to ensure you conclude training with imagery at normal speed which can carry over into competition.

NB: Always finish an imagery exercise at normal speed and remember to record and evaluate the effectiveness each time you use imagery.

EXERCISE 6

DEVELOPING EXTERNAL AND INTERNAL IMAGERY CONTROL

Both external and internal imagery can be very powerful tools. Learn to use both and to be able to switch from one to the other.

6.1 To practise external imagery, choose a simple skill and ask someone to demonstrate it competently for you (or use a video of yourself). Observe the execution from a close side view (or the video) and then immediately close your eyes and try to visualise the entire action from the same external perspective. Repeat this sequence of observation followed by external imagery several times until you can clearly visualise the entire skill at normal speed and in full colour. Always record and evaluate the effectiveness each time you use imagery.

6.2 Choose another fairly simple technique, execute it and note the key visual focus (eg the ball, a piece of sporting equipment, another player, the end of the beam). Immediately close your eyes and try to visualise exactly the technique but seen from an internal perspective during the execution of the technique. Assess the effectiveness of your imagery.

Repeat the physical technique but this time focus on how your body feels as it moves – to give a clearer kinesthetic feel of the movement, it may help to close your eyes (only if safe to do so) or use weighted equipment (eg weighted balls, two tennis rackets, a heavier cricket bat to force the muscles to work harder) so enhancing the kinesthetic feelings. Assess the effectiveness of your imagery.

6.3 Imagine you are in a local weight training room, preparing to do some strength work. Imagine that one exercise will be a biceps curl with a 10kg dumb-bell weight (adapt the weight appropriate to the weight you would normally use). Close your eyes and imagine the dumb-bell securely gripped in your preferred hand and supported either from a curling bench or in your other hand. Imagine the exertion in the flexor muscles of your wrist and biceps as you slowly curl the dumb-bell up toward your shoulder. Feel the tension in your forearm and biceps as you lift the dumb-bell higher. As you lower it from your shoulder, feel the effort in your triceps muscle. Focus your attention on the feelings of the exertion in your muscles. Repeat this mental curl in your mind several times and emphasise feeling the muscular sensations of tension and exertion in the various muscle groups. Always record and evaluate the effectiveness each time you use imagery.

This error correction exercise will help you practise switching from one perspective to another (external – internal). Select a technique in which you are trying to eradicate an error – perhaps a frequent error in the toss up on a tennis serve, a problem just before contact on the golf drive, an error as you enter the tumble turn in the backstroke. Use external imagery to replay the technique and try to spot the problem. Rehearse the technique and notice when it is correct and when the error creeps in. You may need to use correct demonstrations or videos of other performers to judge your execution. Once you have isolated the execution problem, use kinesthetic-based internal imagery to feel what the movement is like when it is incorrect and then when it is correct. Try to execute the correct movement physically and then close your eyes and use internal imagery to feel the correct movement. Replay the correct feeling several times until it is well established. Alternate physical practice and correct internal imagery. Assess the effectiveness of your imagery.

EXERCISE 7

DEVELOPING SENSORY, EMOTIONAL AND OUTCOME IMAGERY

The most effective imagery makes you feel as if you were actually performing the skills. Learn to include as many sensory perceptions and emotional experiences as possible.

7.1

Look back at Exercise 1 (page 22) when you tried to peel an orange or Exercise 2 (page 31) when you imagined the training venue. Try again imagining the:

- feel of a sports object or piece of training equipment
- smell of the changing room, the first aid room or simply the venue
- taste of sweat in the middle of a hard training session or competition
- sound of a sports object (eg crack of the cricket bat, starter's pistol) or the noise of the crowd.

Always record and evaluate the effectiveness each time you use imagery.

7.2

Recall out loud a competitive situation where you experienced the happiness and excitement of a successful performance. Use plenty of feeling and action verbs and adverbs. See if you can imagine the same positive feeling over again. If you are with other people, they might notice emotional signs on your face – for example, happy lines around the eyes and mouth. Try the same exercise recalling a negative occasion – perhaps pre-match anxiety, the anger felt after being viciously fouled by an opponent, the frustration of being called for a foul you did not cause, the disappointment of losing a particularly hard fought match. Again look for evidence (eg ask a friend or use a mirror) of worry lines or sad lines in your face as you re-experience this emotion. Assess the effectiveness of your imagery.

> **NB: This type of exercise can help you experience fully the emotions of competition so you do not have to cope with actual emotions of competition that can overwhelm you.**

7.3

Select a simple task in which you can readily image a successful execution and positive result (eg an ace first serve in tennis, a long one-putt in golf, a perfect clearance of a jump, a successful header for a goal in soccer). Ideally use a video clip of yourself executing this successful action or stop in training immediately after you have achieved this.

Imagine being inside your body and seeing through your eyes (internal perspective) as you visualise a successful execution of the task and feel the sensations of movement. If you have just physically performed the task correctly, try to recreate and imagine how it felt and experience the exaltation and excitement (positive emotions) that accompany the successful execution. Try this several times until you find it easy to imagine a positive outcome to the task and the rewarding feelings that accompany it.

Next, attempt a coping image to overcome a poor performance or feeling. Imagine making a mistake in a competition, or performing poorly in the beginning, or feeling exceptionally anxious. Use action verbs and feeling adverbs to describe how badly you feel. Imagine the negative emotion interfering with performance. Take a deep breath, clear your mind and imagine yourself coping successfully with the situation. For example, a nervous golfer might experience a calming, confident feeling just before she makes a smooth swing and hits a long drive in the middle of the fairway off the first tee. Or a football defender failing to stop a striker, can imagine concentrating more closely on the player, quickly reading the move, taking the right defensive action and smoothly knocking the ball away. Or a runner who was feeling tight and struggling in the first lap might feel her muscles relaxing, her breathing becoming stronger and more regular, her energy level increasing and the rhythm of her pace accelerating.

NB: Remember to use action verbs and feeling adverbs to enhance the clarity and realistic processing of the image in your mind.

7.4 Practise imaging the calming and focusing and then the perfect execution. Gradually introduce this into training and then competition. Always record and evaluate the effectiveness each time you use imagery.

EXERCISE 8

DEVELOPING AND USING AN IMAGERY SCRIPT

To maximise the effects of imagery on learning and performance, you must plan the content carefully. This involves writing individualised scripts to use in training.

8.1

The first step in script writing is to tell the basic story. Select a sport skill or event (such as an action in a match, a strategy in a competition, an outcome in a competition, a pre-match routine) and tell the basic story by outlining the components or behaviours that make up the scene or action in its normal sequence of occurrence (column one).

Step Two is to add more details – add appropriate adjectives and descriptors to each component or behaviour. Use your actual training or competitive facilities or equipment to include as many of the sensory details (eg colours, directions, weights of objects, qualities of noises, smells, feelings) involved in real training or competition. Don't be afraid to add several sensory details to one behaviour if it more accurately describes the event or action.

Add details about the actions and emotions to make the script read as if you were really performing the task or experiencing the event. The more vividly and powerfully the actions and emotions are portrayed, the more valuable the script – be as creative and descriptive as you can.

Step Three involves re-scripting the components or actions into a flowing paragraph you can read easily and clearly – read it to yourself and try to imagine the event in all its sensory, action and emotional detail. See if you feel as if you are actually performing the skill or experiencing the event. If it works successfully for you, you should be able to use it effectively in training sessions and competitions. You may need to add additional adjectives or stronger kinesthetic verbs and adverbs if the images are not perceived as vivid or lifelike. Modify it as necessary until it works for you. You can then use it to practise the skill, prepare to use it at a particular time, or use it successfully in a pressure situation.

> NB: Use the table on the opposite page as a guide or refer back to Exercise 7.3 (page 40) for guidance on how to add descriptors which build vivid and powerful images and emotions.

Table 5: Developing a script for a 100m athlete

Step 1: Telling the Basic Story	Step 2: Adding the Details		Step 3: Refining the Script
	Descriptors	Action/Emotional Words	
1 Getting ready	Excited, nervous, confident, aware of crowd.	Feel excited but energized, nervous but confident in my ability, I hear the crowd buzzing.	I am getting ready for the start of the final in the 100 metres sprint. I am excited but energized, nervous but confident in my ability.
2 Onto starting blocks, position feet and fingers	Place left foot, shake right leg and place right foot on block, fingers to the line, adjust weight.	Purposefully position my left foot in first, and then vigorously shaking my right leg before placing that foot accurately into the blocks. Carefully place fingers behind the starting line ready to push my weight forward onto them.	I hear the crowd buzzing as I settle into the starting blocks, purposefully positioning my left foot in first, and then vigorously shaking my right leg before I place that foot accurately into the blocks. I carefully place my fingers behind the starting line so I can push my weight forward onto them.
3 Focus thoughts	Focus on finish line, deep breaths, think of *explode,* block out sights and sounds, prepare for gun.	Focus down the track at finish line, seeing my lane like a tunnel through which I'll speed. Take deep breaths and tell myself to explode out of the blocks. Unaware of sounds and others; focus on bursting out at the sound of the gun.	I focus on and clearly see the finish line down the track, seeing my lane like a tunnel through which I'll speed. I take two deep breaths and tell myself just to explode out of the blocks. I cannot hear or see the competitors next to me; I am just thinking about bursting out at the sound of the gun.
4 On ready, prepare to move out the block	Make legs feel like coiled springs ready to uncoil, weight further over hands, extend head.	On ready, arch up and compress legs into two coiled springs, shift my weight over my hands and extend my head up.	I hear the command for ready; I arch up and compress my legs into two coiled springs, shift my weight over my hands, and extend my head up.
5 Shot – drive off the blocks	Gun – extend legs fast, start low, pump arms, drive forward.	On gun, extend right leg quickly and forcefully through my arms and stay bent at the waist as legs and arms vigorously pump forward together to generate enormous forward acceleration.	The shot rings out and my right leg extends quickly and forcefully through my arms and I stay bent at the waist as my legs and arms vigorously pump forward together to generate enormous forward acceleration.
6 Into my running	Smooth, up onto toes, drive forward, great pace.	Smoothly onto my toes at top speed, slicing forward at incredibly fast pace.	Within 10 metres, I am gliding on my toes at top speed, slicing forward at incredibly fast pace.

SECTION THREE
Exercises to Use your Imagery Skills

Introduction

Once you have developed your ability to use imagery effectively, you can use imagery to develop, refine and maintain skills, to rehearse strategies and decision-making and to improve other mental qualities such as commitment, control, confidence and concentration. In this section, six exercises have been developed to help you use your imagery skills for specific purposes to enhance training and improve your performance in competition.

EXERCISE 9
USING IMAGERY FOR SKILL DEVELOPMENT AND MAINTENANCE

Once you have developed your ability to use imagery effectively, you can employ imagery rehearsal regularly for remembering movement feelings, practising perfect execution and correcting errors.

9.1 Select a skill or aspect of training where imagery would be a useful additional form of rehearsal. Schedule the imagery training into your daily practice routine in a 10–20 minute session or as alternating minute-long imagery breaks where you can use the imagery to practise a skill or strategy as mental training. Plan how you will use it in your training sessions for the forthcoming week.

> NB: Rehearse it regularly during quiet times outside training (eg while travelling, before bed, as a break from work, in the bath or shower). Remember that mental imagery should be practised for 10–15 minutes every day outside training. Recording and evaluating your imagery sessions (see Appendix C, page 62) will also ensure it continues to prove effective.

9.2 A number of exercises have already been described which use imagery to identify and correct errors. You are recommended to use the following:

- Exercise 4 (page 35) which emphasises the value of working through the three stages of observation (demonstration), physical practice and imagery. It also recommends the benefits of using video playback to provide the physical demonstration of the correct action.

- Exercise 5.2 (page 37) which utilises slow motion video playback with imagery to correct errors.

- Exercise 7.3 (page 40) which employs external imagery to replay the technique to identify the error and then kinesthetic-based internal imagery to differentiate between the correct and incorrect movements.

9.3 Further ideas and developments can be found in Section Four (page 51).

EXERCISE 10
USING IMAGERY TO IMPROVE DECISION-MAKING

Once you have developed your ability to use imagery effectively, start to use it to learn and rehearse sport strategies, for cue focus, decision-making or problem solving.

10.1

Select a situation in your sport in which you have to make decisions. For example, if you play a racket game, you might identify a situation in which you have to select the right stroke to play (eg the type of serve or return, drop shot or deep drive, to backhand or forehand, follow it in or stay back). If you are involved in a team game such as hockey, soccer or rugby, you might choose a 3-on-2 passing situation. Your decision is to select the right pass to an open team-mate. You need to use internal imagery to see the situation through your own eyes – your own position, the position of other players, the ball. Make it as vivid and real as possible. Make the decision and see yourself execute it successfully. Assess your imagery effectiveness.

If you found this difficult, repeat it several times. List some of the cues you would use to help you make the decision. In the racket game, it might be the speed and trajectory of the ball, the position of your opponent on the court, the weather or court conditions, the score line. In the team game example, the cues might include the distance of the defender from your team-mate, the distance between you and your team-mates, how closely your defender is marking you, how fast your team-mates are moving, the amount of space around your team-mates.

Imagery may provide additional training time for performers to rehearse this cue recognition so they can more quickly and efficiently process the information, make the right decisions and produce an automated successful result.

10.2

Further ideas and developments can be found in Section Four (page 51).

EXERCISE 11
USING IMAGERY
TO STRENGTHEN
COMMITMENT

Once you have developed your ability to use imagery effectively, start to use it to strengthen commitment.

11.1 Examine your short- and long-term goals for the season and write an imagery script based on one of these. For example, you might choose to image achieving a specific time, place (eg top three), distance or score in a race or event, a perfect execution of a skill or routine, a specific target behaviour that represents a short-term goal step towards a long-term goal or just visually seeing the goal written out in your mind's eye. Use the three-step approach explained in Exercise 8 and ensure you include as many of the senses as possible involved in the image (eg the roar of the crowd on victory), strong kinesthetic sensations (eg feeling your body move and muscles exert to accomplish the goal) and several emotions (eg the thrill of victory or exhilaration of success). Try the image in training – check the effectiveness of the image before using it prior to a specific competition.

11.2 Further ideas and developments can be found in Section Four (page 51).

EXERCISE 12
USING IMAGERY TO IMPROVE CONCENTRATION

Once you have developed your ability to use imagery effectively, start to use it to improve concentration.

12.1

Draw up a set of concentration cues for pre-competition and competition routines[1]. For example, you might:

- select imagery cue words or triggers to prime the execution of specific skills (eg smooth golf swing, kick through the spot in kicking sports, knees-toes-and-in for basketball free throw shooting)

- practise competitive images of reading cues for decision-making (eg a soccer or basketball player quickly assessing the opponent's defensive positions and team-mates' offensive positions to decide whether to dribble, pass or shoot)

- focus on details in the environment at certain times in a competition (eg the pebbly feel of a basketball, the firm grip on a racket) or yourself (eg muscle tension in one part of your body, your heart rate)

- practise images to cope with the pain of exertion (eg for endurance athletes) or minor injuries when competing in a high intensity race (eg focusing on positive thoughts or the finish line during the pain of the final kick or sprint for home).

Then list all the possible problems and distractions that could occur before and during competition and create refocusing cues to help you return to the sport task. Before practice matches and mock competitions, mentally rehearse these cues. Make sure you imagine yourself using the cue, focusing on the sport skill and then its successful execution. Then begin to do this for several nights before the real competition.

Try using the focusing cues in your pre-competitive and competitive routines for several competitions. Evaluate the effectiveness and revise the cues if necessary.

NB: Regularly mentally rehearse using both the focusing and refocusing cues prior to forthcoming competitions.

12.2

Further ideas and developments can be found in Section Four (page 51).

---

1   For further information on the use of routines in this context, you are recommended to refer to the **sports coach UK** resource, *Improving Concentration*, available from **Coachwise 1st4sport** (tel 0113-201 5555 or visit www.1st4sport.com).

EXERCISE 13

USING IMAGERY
TO BUILD
SELF-CONFIDENCE

*Mental imagery can be particularly
powerful for creating self-confidence.
Once you have developed your ability
to use imagery effectively, start to use
it to build self-confidence.*

13.1

Choose a skill in which you would like to be more confident and try to imagine successfully executing this skill or event by imagining:

- the perfect execution of the skill (mastery image)
- overcoming an obstacle or difficulty during performance and finally succeeding in the task (coping images).

Select a positive self statement or cue (eg 'I know I can make this putt, keep your head still') to accompany the rehearsal of the image in training and prior to competition[1].

Write an imagery script using the three-step approach and as many sensory images, kinesthetic sensations and emotions as you can. Check the effectiveness and start to use prior to training, then mock and low level competitions and finally before major events. Always record and evaluate the effectiveness each time you use imagery.

Some of the ideas in Exercise 18 (page 55) may also be useful building self-confidence.

13.2

Further ideas and developments can be found in Section Four (page 51).

---

1   For further information on positive self statements, you are recommended to refer to the **sports coach UK** resource, *Building Self-confidence,* available from **Coachwise 1st4sport** (tel 0113-201 5555 or visit www.1st4sport.com).

EXERCISE 14

IMAGERY TO CONTROL EMOTIONS AND HANDLE PRESSURE

Imagery can be used to control anxiety or to raise the level to help you achieve your ideal performance state.

14.1

Once you have established your own ideal performance state (IPS)[1] and recognised the situations that create anxiety, you can use imagery as part of a relaxation strategy (imagery-based relaxation) or as a coping mechanism (imagining successfully dealing with the situation).

Write an imagery script using the three-step approach and ensure you:

• use kinesthetic-based images of being relaxed and feeling in control

• imagine yourself first struggling with anxiety but then successfully coping and performing to your best (ie coping images)

• record and evaluate the effectiveness each time you use imagery.

Similarly, if you recognise you need to elevate your arousal level, imagery can be used to achieve your IPS. Once again use the three-step approach to write an imagery script including:

• kinesthetic-based images associated with the appropriate level of arousal

• imagining the inappropriate arousal level and then successfully elevating your arousal and performing to your best (ie coping images)

• recording and evaluating the effectiveness each time you use imagery.

Exercise 7.3 (page 41) might be a useful one to practise using imagery to cope with difficult situations such as in dealing with a mistake, poor form or anxiety.

14.2

Further ideas and developments can be found in Section Four (page 51).

---

1   For further information, you are recommended to refer to the **sports coach UK** resource, *Handling Pressure*, available from **Coachwise 1st4sport** (tel 0113-201 5555 or visit www.1st4sport.com).

SECTION FOUR
Exercises to Build Imagery into Training and Competition

Introduction

Imagery must be practised regularly and in conjunction with normal training sessions if it is to affect the performance outcome positively. It should be included in every training session even if for only a few minutes. It can also be practised outside training (eg while travelling, in the bath or shower, as a break from work, while waiting for the kettle to boil). Recommended schedules for imagery work for those with limited or no experience of using imagery usually include introductory education about imagery, imagery ability assessment, imagery rehearsal of basic sport skills and relaxation imagery for pre-season (ie work based on Exercises 1–8). Once the basic skills have been learnt, pre-season work should include relaxation imagery, rehearsal of simple and complex skills and strategies, as well as imagery work on developing the important mental qualities: commitment, concentration, confidence and control (ie work based on Exercises 9–14). This kind of work can continue into the competitive season, together with imagery of competitive strategies. Before competitions, you should practise imagery-based pre-competitive and competitive routines and, as the season progresses and more important competitions occur, you can revise imagery scripts to meet the special pressures and requirements of elite competitions. Even in the off-season, you can use imagery training to begin programming yourself toward certain goals and even additions or improvements to skills you wish to undertake for the next season.

In this section, you will find exercises to help you build imagery into your weekly training sessions and your annual plan. There are also specific exercises to help you use it in the real life competition environment.

EXERCISE 15

INCORPORATING IMAGERY INTO WEEKLY TRAINING

Imagery should be included in every training session – even if only for a few minutes – as well as regularly outside training.

15.1 Select one of your weekly training plans used during the competitive season. For each day of the week, write down at least one imagery training exercise that can be related to current practice techniques and find 10–15 minutes to schedule it into your practice (and before competition if you have one). In addition, identify imagery practice for use at home away from training – while travelling, in the bath or shower, as a break from work, while waiting for the kettle to boil. Select relevant activities from the large number of exercises you have undertaken in Section Three of this pack. Try each activity in daily training.

Day	Activities	Homework	Evaluation
Sunday			
Monday			
Tuesday			
Wednesday			
Thursday			
Friday			
Saturday			

Weekly Training Schedule

Using the sample forms in Appendix C (page 62), assess the usefulness of each activity and use this to plan the forthcoming week's imagery training work.

EXERCISE 16

INCORPORATING
IMAGERY
INTO THE
ANNUAL PLAN

You can plan to use imagery for different purposes throughout the training year – in the pre-season to programme goals for the forthcoming season or to work on technique training to enhance physical and mental skills, as well as before, during and after competitions.

16.1

Once you have some experience of using imagery in every day training sessions, you can begin to plan how you will incorporate it across the whole competitive year. Select exercises from this pack (or indeed from any other book on imagery) that would be appropriate for the off-season, pre-season training and competitive season training. List these in the following planning log and attempt to use them systematically for the next competitive year.

Pre-season imagery activities (for training)	
Competitive season imagery activities (for training and competition)	
Off-season imagery activities (for out of training)	

Competitive Year Plan

EXERCISE 17
USING IMAGERY AT CRITICAL MOMENTS

Successful elite athletes use imagery at critical moments to cope with uncertainty and competitive stress.

17.1 Using the five critical moments referred to on page 20 (Hardy and Fazey 1990), select specific situations for using imagery for practice and competition and identify the purpose of each.

Critical Moment	Situation	Purpose
Performance rehearsal before, during and after training or practice		
Instant preview before competition		
Preview during performance or competition		
Instant review during competition		
Performance review after competition		

Select one of the critical moment situations and write an imagery script for it. If the content of the image involves skill performance, consider using videotape examples of good and poor performance to help identify areas of the execution on which to focus for improvement.

Try out the script in a regular training session, then a low level or simulated competition. Check the effectiveness of the imagery in terms of vividness, content and control. Ensure there is plenty of kinesthetic sensation and appropriate emotion. Use the imagery assessment form if helpful (Appendix C on page 62). Evaluate and refine the script as necessary.

Finally use the script in high level competition and remember to record and evaluate the effectiveness each time you use imagery.

17.2 Repeat the procedure for each of the other critical moments.

EXERCISE 18

USING IMAGERY IN COMPETITION ROUTINES

Successful elite athletes practise and use pre-competitive and competitive routines to cope with the stress and uncertainty of competition. Imagery rehearsal forms a large part of these routines.

18.1 Select the script you have written for the instant preview situation (Exercise 17). It may have included relaxing images, rehearsal of simple or complex sport skills, rehearsal of a competitive strategy, imagining past successes or programming a desired goal for success. Some athletes like to use several images during their warm-up and immediately before competition. For example, some racers imagine their race strategy during stretching and early warm-up. Later, immediately before the race is about to start, they use a simple image of successful time or place joined with a cue word to enhance their confidence. Alternatively, they imagine how they want to perform at the start of the race or the first segment.

18.2 Select one or more of the image contents you want to incorporate into your pre-competition routine – if you are a golfer, it might be a relaxing image to help you stay loose, followed by a rehearsal of your swing cued by repeating a cue word like smooth; if you are a team player, you might rehearse a play or strategy. Practise rehearsing the image and revise the script if necessary.

18.3 Practise the pre-competition routine before a competition in training (a scrimmage or mock competition) and in the warm-up before friendly competitions. Ensure it becomes a habitual part of the warm-up and then begin to use it before all competitions. Evaluate it and refine the script as necessary.

18.4 Identify natural breaks in competition where you could use quick imagery rehearsal – for example mentally rehearsing the proper execution of a skill (eg at a penalty), a strategy (eg playing the first volley) or a play (eg at a corner or re-start when the ball has gone out of play). Refer back to your preview during performance critical moment script (Exercise 17) and revise it for use within a routine to use in a natural break in competition. You may wish to use cue words to remind you of a kinesthetic feeling or a particular component of the skill execution.

It is also valuable to do the same thing with the instant review scripts, for routines can be developed to cope with replaying skills or strategies after its completion – after to reinforce the correct movement or to identify the error and then rehearse the correct movement.

Rehearse the script several times to ensure it works as expected and make any necessary adjustments. Use it first in training and gradually progress to trying them in low level and finally high level competitions. Always evaluate the effectiveness and be prepared to adjust the scripts whenever necessary.

18.5

Performance review allows you to replay good and bad parts of the competition to identify areas of future training, correct mistakes and build self-confidence for the future. You need to develop and use a post-competitive routine to do this. Review and rehearse your script, revise it to make it more relevant or more effective as necessary. Try it after simulated competitions and actual competitions. You might develop the habit of doing this at a specific time – for example in the bath or shower, on the way home, before going to sleep at night.

Good portions of performance should be rehearsed so you feel proud of your accomplishments and so build self-confidence. Mistakes should be mentally rehearsed to identify where they occurred in execution and then the perfect execution should be rehearsed – always finish with the correct execution.

Final Summary

If you have worked conscientiously through this pack, you should now have a good understanding of the art and science of using imagery training. You have learnt what it is, how to use it in training and competition to enhance performance, and when and where to use it in practice and competition. The best athletes in the world in every sport use imagery to improve performance in training and competition – but it works with novice athletes as well as elite professionals. It takes only regular practice, proper instruction and good effort to bring positive results to performance.

Imagery is also a powerful life skill that can be used to enhance other mental qualities (concentration, commitment, confidence and control) and so the quality of life at home, school, work and play. It can help you take better control of your life. Anything you can imagine in detail, you can do.

References and Further Reading

Bacon, T. (1988) *Periodisation of Mental Skills Training.* Ottawa: Coaching Association of Canada (out of print).

Bull, S., Albinson, J. and Shambrook, C. (1996) 'Visualisation'. In *The Mental Game Plan: Getting Psyched for Sport,* pp 65–84. Eastbourne: Fitness Dynamics. ISBN: 0-951954-32-6.

*Butler, R. (1996) *Performance Profiling* (audiotape and book) Leeds: The National Coaching Foundation. ISBN: 0-947850-36-8.

Hale, B.D. (1982) 'The effects of internal and external imagery on muscular and ocular concomitants'. *Journal of Sport Psychology,* 4, pp 379–387.

Hardy, L. and Fazey, J. (1990) *Mental Rehearsal* (audiotape and book) Leeds: The National Coaching Foundation. ISBN: 0-947850-71-6 (out of print).

*Harwood, C. (1998) *Handling Pressure.* Leeds: The National Coaching Foundation. ISBN: 0-902523-09-1.

*Maynard, I. (1998) *Improving Concentration.* Leeds: The National Coaching Foundation. ISBN: 1-902523-01-6.

Murphy, S. and Jowdy, D. (1992) 'Imagery and mental practice'. T Horn (Ed) *Advances in Sport Psychology (2nd Edition)* Champaign IL: Human Kinetics, pp 221–250. ISBN: 0-736032-98-3.

Orlick, T. (1986) *Psyching for Sport: Mental Training for Athletes.* Champaign IL: Human Kinetics (out of print).

Orlick, T. (1990) *In Pursuit of Excellence: How to Win in Sport and Life Through Mental Training* (3rd Edition). Champaign IL: Human Kinetics. ISBN: 0-736031-86-3.

Orlick, T. and Partington, J. (1988) 'Mental links to excellence'. *The Sport Psychologist,* 2, pp 105–130.

* Sellars, C. (1997) *Building Self-confidence.* Leeds: The National Coaching Foundation. ISBN: 0-947850-11-2.

* Sellars, C. (1996) *Mental Skills: An Introduction for Sports Coaches.* Leeds: The National Coaching Foundation. ISBN: 0-947850-34-1.

Suinn, R.M. (1993) 'Mental imagery'. In R. Singer, M. Murphey and K. Tennant (Eds.) *Handbook of Research in Sport Psychology.* New York: Macmillan (out of print).

Vealey, R. and Walter, S. (1993) 'Imagery training for performance enhancement and personal development'. In J.M. Williams (Ed.) *Applied Sport Psychology: Personal Growth to Peak Performance* (4th edition) pp 200–224. Mountain View, CA: Mayfield Publ. ISBN: 0-767417-47-X.

* Available from **Coachwise** 1st4sport (0113-201 5555).

APPENDIX A
Useful Contacts

For details of all **sports coach UK** workshops in England, please contact the **sports coach UK** Business Support Centre on 01509-226130 or email bsc@sportscoachuk.org or, alternatively, visit the **sports coach UK** website www.sportscoachuk.org

sports coach UK

114 Cardigan Road
Headingley
Leeds LS6 3BJ
Tel: 0113-274 4802
Fax: 0113-275 5019
Email: coaching@sportscoachuk.org
Website: www.sportscoachuk.org

For **sports coach UK** workshops in Wales, Northern Ireland and Scotland please contact the appropriate office, details of which are below:

Sports Council for Wales

Sophia Gardens
Cardiff CF11 9SW
Tel: 029-2030 0500
Fax: 029-2030 0600
Email: publicity@scw.co.uk
Website: www.sports-council-wales.co.uk

Coaching Northern Ireland

Queens Physical Education Centre
Botanic Gardens
Belfast BT9 5EX
Tel: 02890-686940
Fax: 02890-666119
Email: information@coachingni.net
Website: www.coachingni.net

sportscotland

Caledonia House
South Gyle
Edinburgh EH12 9DQ
Tel: 0131-317 7200
Fax: 0131-317 7202
Email: library@sportscotland.org.uk
Website: www.sportscotland.org.uk

APPENDIX B
Assessment and
Monitoring Form

This form might be used for an initial assessment and then every two or three months to monitor progress against your goals.

1   Using a 10-point scale (1= not at all and 10 = perfect), rate your current and ideal score on each of the qualities of imagery described on the perimeter of the following chart:

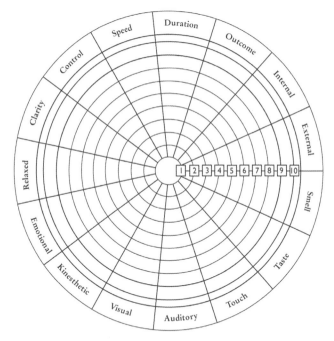

2   You may also wish to profile your ability to use imagery in different situations. Using the same ten point scale, rate your current and ideal scores for each of the imagery uses on the following chart:

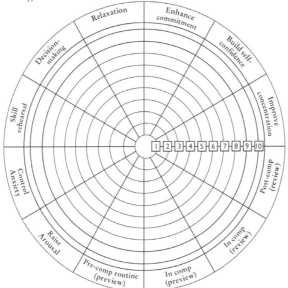

3   Look at the differences between ideal and current scores on each profile and prioritise the area(s) in which you feel an improvement would make a significant difference to your ability to use imagery in training and competition.

4   Write an action plan using process goals (to improve score by x), selecting relevant exercises from this pack or other books to show how and when you will develop your imagery skills:

Action plan
Priority areas:

Process goal:

Selected exercises:

Time frame for implementation/reassessment on:

APPENDIX C: Evaluation Form

You may wish to use some of the rating scales on this form to help you evaluate your imagery skills following an exercise or use of imagery in competition:

Name:		Date:
Time:	Place:	

Attribute	Rating scale	Comments
Level of relaxation	very somewhat perfectly uptight relaxed relaxed 1 2 3 4 5 6 7 8 9 10	
Visual content	can't see somewhat vivid perfectly anything and accurate accurate 1 2 3 4 5 6 7 8 9 10	
Auditory content	can't hear somewhat vivid perfectly anything and accurate accurate 1 2 3 4 5 6 7 8 9 10	
Touch content	can't feel somewhat vivid perfectly anything and accurate accurate 1 2 3 4 5 6 7 8 9 10	
Kinesthetic content	can't feel somewhat vivid perfectly anything and accurate accurate 1 2 3 4 5 6 7 8 9 10	
Smell content	can't smell somewhat vivid perfectly anything and accurate accurate 1 2 3 4 5 6 7 8 9 10	
Taste content	can't taste somewhat vivid perfectly anything and accurate accurate 1 2 3 4 5 6 7 8 9 10	
General sensory content	no sensory somewhat vivid perfectly images and accurate accurate 1 2 3 4 5 6 7 8 9 10	
Internal control	no internal some perfect control control control 1 2 3 4 5 6 7 8 9 10	
External control	no external some perfect control control control 1 2 3 4 5 6 7 8 9 10	
Emotional content	no some perfect emotion emotion emotion 1 2 3 4 5 6 7 8 9 10	
Effectiveness of script	not somewhat perfectly effective effective effective 1 2 3 4 5 6 7 8 9 10